Alfred's

Kid's Ukulele Course 1

Ages 5 and Up

The Easiest Ukulele Method Ever!

Ron Manus • L. C. Harnsberger

Special thanks to our families and friends, and especially to Jennifer, Genevieve, Patrese, and Catherine Harnsberger.

Alfred Music Publishing Co., Inc.
P.O. Box 10003
Van Nuys, CA 91410-0003
alfred.com

ISBN-10: 0-7390-7083-5, ISBN-13: 978-0-7390-7083-3 (Book & CD)
ISBN-10: 0-7390-7082-7, ISBN-13: 978-0-7390-7082-6 (Book, CD & DVD)
ISBN-10: 0-7390-7084-3, ISBN-13: 978-0-7390-7084-0 (DVD)

Cover and interior illustrations by Jeff Shelly.
Ukulele photo courtesy of Martin Guitars.
Photos on page 6 by Jennifer Harnsberger Photography, jhphotostudio.com.

D1441646

Contents

Selecting Your Ukulele

Ukuleles come in different types and sizes. There are four basic sizes: soprano, concert, tenor, and baritone. The smallest is the soprano, and they get gradually bigger, with the baritone being the largest.

| Soprano | Concert | Tenor | Baritone |

Soprano, concert, and tenor ukes are all tuned to the same notes, but the baritone is tuned to different notes. Each uke has a different sound. The soprano has a light, soft sound, which is what you expect when you hear a ukulele. The larger the instrument, the deeper the sound is. Some tenor ukuleles have six or even eight strings.

The soprano ukulele is the most common, but you can use soprano, concert, and four-string tenor ukuleles with this book. Because the baritone uke is tuned to the same notes as the top four strings of the guitar, you can use *Alfred's Kid's Guitar Method Book 1* to start learning on that type of ukulele.

Parts of the Ukulele

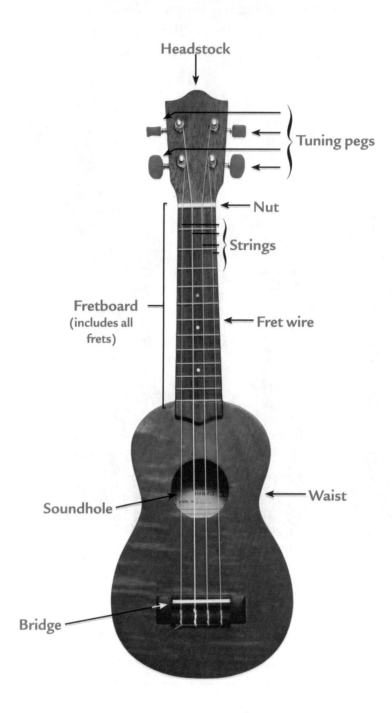

Headstock

Tuning pegs

Nut

Strings

Fretboard
(includes all
frets)

Fret wire

Soundhole

Waist

Bridge

Caring for Your Ukulele

Get to know your ukulele and treat it like a friend. When you carry it, think of it as part of your body so you don't accidentally bump it against walls or furniture, and be especially sure not to drop it! Every time you are done playing, carefully dust off your ukulele with a soft cloth, and be sure to put it away in its case. If you don't have a case, always put it in a safe place where it won't be in the way.

Tuning Your Ukulele

First make sure your strings are wound properly around the tuning pegs. They should go from the inside to the outside, as in the picture.

Turning a tuning peg clockwise makes the pitch lower. Turning a tuning peg counter-clockwise makes the pitch higher. Be sure not to tune the strings too high because they could break!

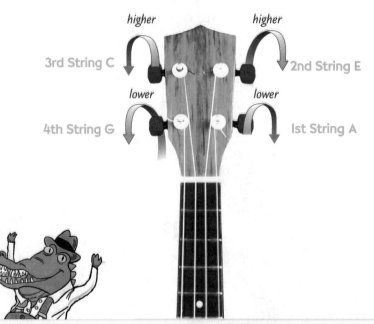

higher   higher

3rd String C   2nd String E

lower   lower

4th String G   1st String A

Important:

Always remember that the string closest to the floor is the first string. The one closest to the ceiling is the fourth string.

Ceiling

Fourth String

Floor

First String

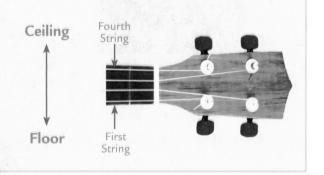

Tuning with the CD or DVD

Tracks 1 & 2

Using Your CD
Put the CD in your CD player and play Tracks 1 and 2. Listen to the directions and match each of your ukulele's strings to its pitch on the CD.

Using Your DVD
Put the DVD in your computer or DVD player. Go to the Scenes menu and click on Tuning. Follow the directions and listen carefully to get your ukulele in tune.

Tuning without the CD or DVD

Tuning the Ukulele to Itself
When your first string is in tune, you can tune the rest of the strings just using the ukulele alone. First tune the first string to A on the piano, then follow the instructions to the right to get the ukulele in tune.

Press fret 5 of string 2 and tune it to the pitch of string 1 (A).

Press fret 4 of string 3 and tune it to the pitch of string 2 (E).

Press fret 2 of string 4 and tune it to the pitch of string 1 (A).

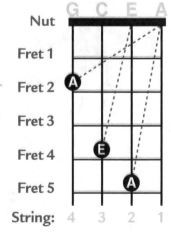

	G	C	E	A
Nut				
Fret 1				
Fret 2		A		
Fret 3				
Fret 4			E	
Fret 5				A
String:	4	3	2	1

Pitch Pipes and Electronic Tuners
If you don't have a piano available, buying an electronic tuner or pitch pipe is recommended. The salesperson at your music store can show you how to use them.

How to Hold Your Ukulele

Hold your ukulele in the position that is most comfortable for you. Some positions are shown below.

Sitting

Rest the ukulele gently on your thigh.

Cradle the ukulele with your right arm by gently holding it close to your body. Your right hand should be free to strum it.

Standing

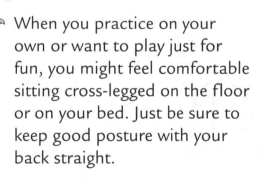

When you practice on your own or want to play just for fun, you might feel comfortable sitting cross-legged on the floor or on your bed. Just be sure to keep good posture with your back straight.

Sitting on the floor

Strumming the Strings

To *strum* means to play the strings with your right hand by brushing quickly across them. There are two common ways of strumming the strings. One is with a pick, and the second is with the fingers.

Strumming with a Pick

Hold the pick between your thumb and index finger. Hold it firmly, but don't squeeze it too hard.

Strum from the fourth string (closest to the ceiling) to the first string (closest to the floor).

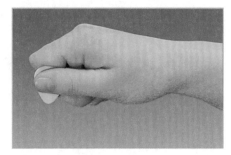

Start near the top string.

Move mostly your wrist, not just your arm. Finish near the bottom string.

Strumming with Your Fingers

First decide if you feel more comfortable strumming with the side of your thumb or the nail of your index finger. The strumming motion is the same with the thumb or finger as it is when using the pick. Strum from the fourth string (closest to the ceiling) to the first string (closest to the floor).

Strumming with the thumb

Strumming with the index finger

Important:

Strum by mostly moving your wrist, not just your arm. Use as little motion as possible. Start as close to the top string as you can, and never let your hand move past the edge of the ukulele.

Track 3

Time to Strum!

Strum all four strings slowly and evenly.
Count your strums out loud as you play.
Repeat this exercise until you feel comfortable strumming the strings.

strum	strum	strum	strum	strum	strum	strum	strum
/	/	/	/	/	/	/	/

Count: 1   2   3   4   5   6   7   8

Strumming Notation

Beats

Each strum you play is equal to one *beat*. Beats are even, like the ticking of a clock.

tick - tick - tick - tick
beat-beat-beat-beat

Introducing the Quarter-Note Slash

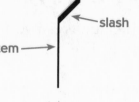

slash

stem

1 beat

A slash with a stem is called a *quarter-note slash*. Each quarter-note slash equals one beat.

The Staff and Treble Clef

Ukulele music is usually written on a five-line *staff* that has a *treble clef* at its beginning.

Treble clef

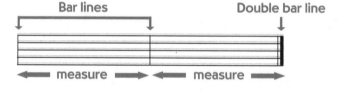

5
4
3
2
1

Bar Lines, Measures, and Time Signatures

Bar lines divide the staff into equal parts called measures. A *double bar line* is used at the end to show you the music is finished.

Bar lines   Double bar line

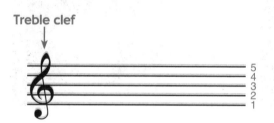

measure   measure

Measures are always filled with a certain number of beats. You know how many beats are in each measure by looking at the *time signature*, which is always at the beginning of the music. A $\frac{4}{4}$ time signature ("four-four time") means there are 4 equal beats in every measure.

Time signature

More Time to Strum

Track 4

Play this example in $\frac{4}{4}$ time. It will sound the same as "Time to Strum," which you played on the previous page. Keep the beats even and count out loud.

Strum all four strings as you did before.

Strum Strum Strum Strum   Strum Strum Strum Strum

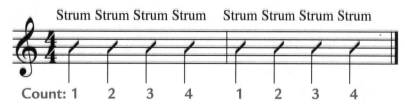

Count: 1   2   3   4   1   2   3   4

Strumming all four strings

8

Using Your Left Hand

Hand Position

Learning to use your left-hand fingers easily starts with a good hand position. Place your hand so your thumb rests comfortably in the middle of the back of the neck. Position your fingers on the front of the neck as if you are gently squeezing a ball between them and your thumb. Keep your elbow in and your fingers curved.

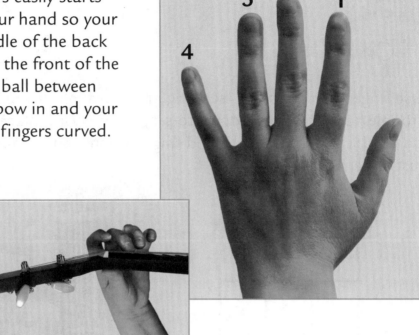

Keep elbow in and fingers curved

Like gently squeezing a ball between your fingertips and thumb

Placing a Finger on a String

When you press a string with a left-hand finger, make sure you press firmly with the tip of your finger and as close to the fret wire as you can without actually being right on it. Short fingernails are important! This will create a clean, bright tone.

RIGHT
Finger presses the string down near the fret without actually being on it.

WRONG
Finger is too far from fret wire; tone is "buzzy" and indefinite.

WRONG
Finger is on top of fret wire; tone is muffled and unclear.

How to Read Chord Diagrams

Chord diagrams show where to place your fingers. The example to the right shows finger 1 on the first string at the first fret. The "o"s above the second, third and fourth strings tell you these strings are to be played open, meaning without pressing down on them with a left-hand finger.

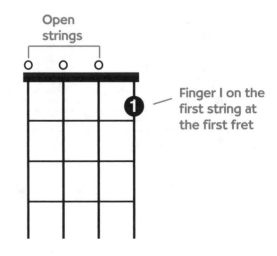

Open strings

Finger 1 on the first string at the first fret

The C Chord

Use finger 3 to press the 1st string at the 3rd fret. If you have any trouble holding finger 3 down to play the C chord, place fingers 1 and 2 on the 1st and 2nd frets behind finger 3 until you are able to play with just finger 3.

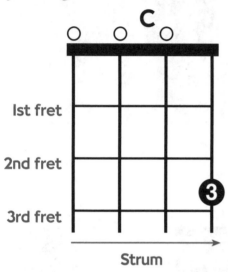

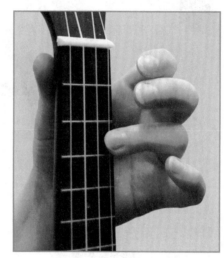

Strumming

Strum the four-string C chord on each quarter-note slash ⌐. Make sure your strums are even. Count aloud as you play:

1–2–3–4 | 1–2–3–4.

Listen to the song on your CD or DVD to hear how it should sound!

My First Chord

 Track 6

Remember: This means there are 4 beats in each measure.

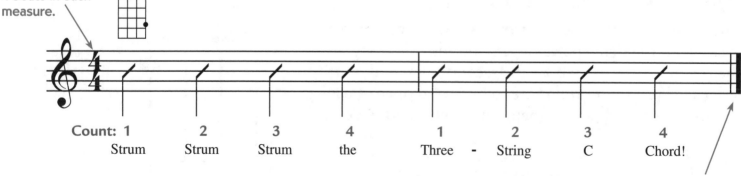

Count: 1   2   3   4   1   2   3   4
        Strum Strum Strum the   Three - String C   Chord!

This **double bar line** tells us the music is finished.

10

The Quarter Rest

Introducing the Quarter Rest

1 beat

This strange-looking music symbol means to be silent for one beat. Stop the sound of the strings by lightly touching them with the side of your hand, as in the photo.

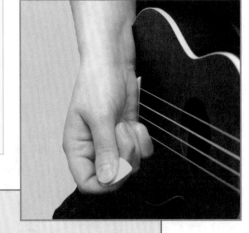

Track 7

Rest Warm-up

Before playing "Three Blind Mice," practice this exercise until you are comfortable playing rests.

| Strum | Strum | Strum | Stop | Strum | Strum | Strum | Stop |

1   2   3   (rest)   1   2   3   (rest)

Practice Tip

Strum the chords and have a friend sing the words.

Three Blind Mice

Track 8   **C**

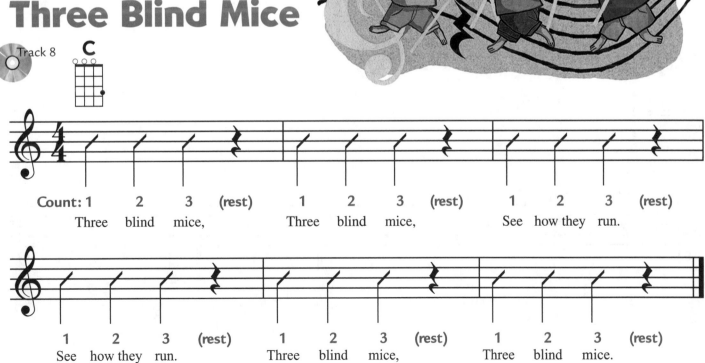

Count: 1   2   3   (rest)   1   2   3   (rest)   1   2   3   (rest)
Three blind mice,   Three blind mice,   See how they run.

1   2   3   (rest)   1   2   3   (rest)   1   2   3   (rest)
See how they run.   Three blind mice,   Three blind mice.

11

The C⁷ Chord

Hear this chord!

Track 9

Use finger 1 to press the 1st string at the 1st fret. This chord is just like the C chord but you are using your 1st finger and not your 3rd finger.

C7

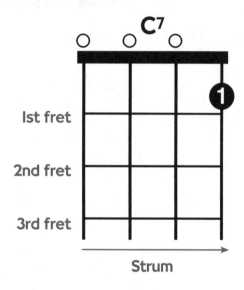

1st fret

2nd fret

3rd fret

Strum

My Second Chord

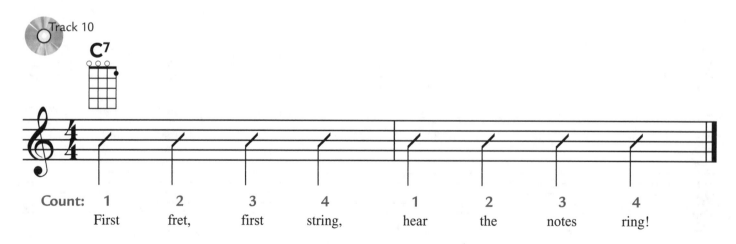

Track 10

C7

Count: 1   2   3   4   1   2   3   4

First   fret,   first   string,   hear   the   notes   ring!

Troubadour Song

Remember to stop the sound by lightly touching
the strings with the side of your hand on each ♩.
Wait one beat.

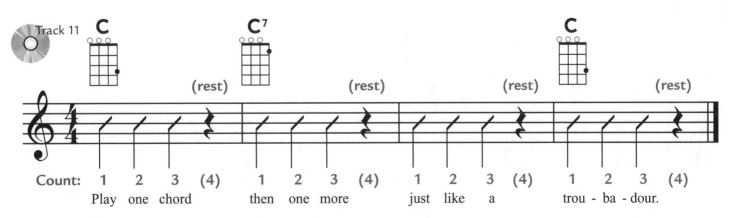

Track 11

C   C⁷   C   C

(rest)   (rest)   (rest)   (rest)

Count: 1 2 3 (4)   1 2 3 (4)   1 2 3 (4)   1 2 3 (4)

Play one chord   then one more   just like a   trou - ba - dour.

*A troubadour was a musician who traveled around singing and playing.

13

The F Chord

Hear this chord! Track 12

This is the first time you are pressing two fingers down at one time. First press finger 1 on the 2nd string at the 1st fret. Then use finger 2 to press the 4th string at the 2nd fret. Press both fingers down firmly as you strum all the strings.

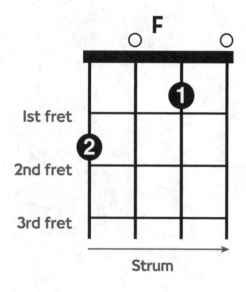

F

1st fret

2nd fret

3rd fret

Strum

My Third Chord

Track 13

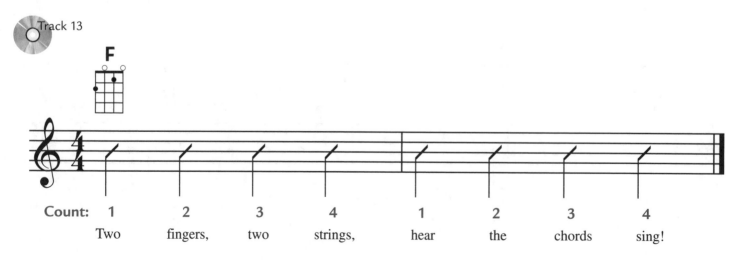

F

Count: 1   2   3   4   1   2   3   4

Two   fingers,   two   strings,   hear   the   chords   sing!

Three Chords in One Song

F   C⁷   C

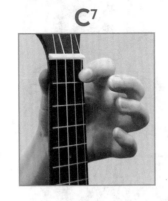
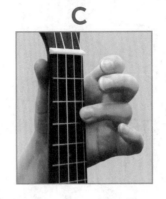

Remember:

This song has three different chords in it. At first, take your time and play slowly so that all the notes sound clearly. Don't forget to be silent for a beat on each quarter rest as you change to a new chord.

Rain Comes Down

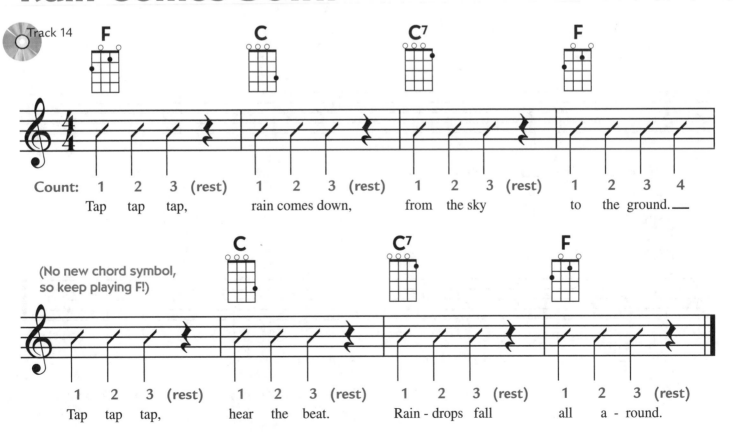

Track 14   F   C   C⁷   F

Count: 1   2   3 (rest)   1   2   3 (rest)   1   2   3 (rest)   1   2   3   4

Tap   tap   tap,   rain comes down,   from   the sky   to   the ground. ___

(No new chord symbol, so keep playing F!)   C   C⁷   F

1   2   3 (rest)   1   2   3 (rest)   1   2   3 (rest)   1   2   3 (rest)

Tap   tap   tap,   hear   the   beat.   Rain - drops   fall   all   a - round.

15

Skip to My Lou

Practice Tip

To change quickly from C⁷ to F in the last two measures, move your 1st finger to the 2nd string—that's not very far—and then put your 2nd finger on the 4th string.

Track 15

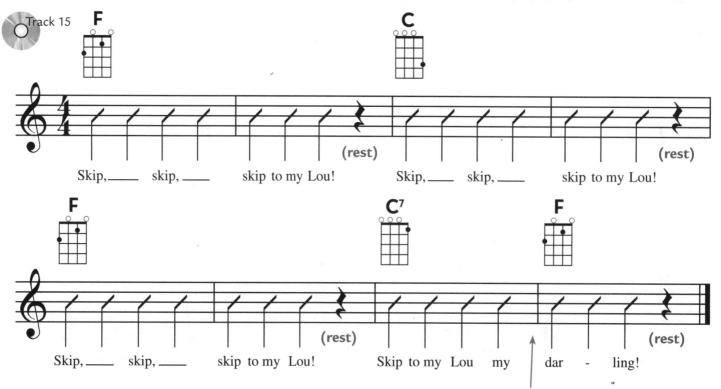

Skip,____ skip, ____ skip to my Lou! (rest) Skip, ____ skip, ____ skip to my Lou! (rest)

Skip, ____ skip, ____ skip to my Lou! (rest) Skip to my Lou my dar - ling! (rest)

Remember to move your 1st finger to the 2nd string and then put your 2nd finger on the 4th string to play the F chord on the next beat.

16

London Bridge

F   C   F

Lon - don Bridge is   fal - ling down,   (rest)   fal - ling down,   (rest)   fal - ling down   (rest)

(No new chord symbol, so keep playing F!) C^7 F

Lon - don Bridge is   fal - ling down,   (rest)   my_____ fair_____   la - dy.   (rest)

The Repeat Sign

Introducing Repeat Dots :|

Double dots on the inside of a double bar line mean to go back to the beginning and play again.

Merrily We Roll Along

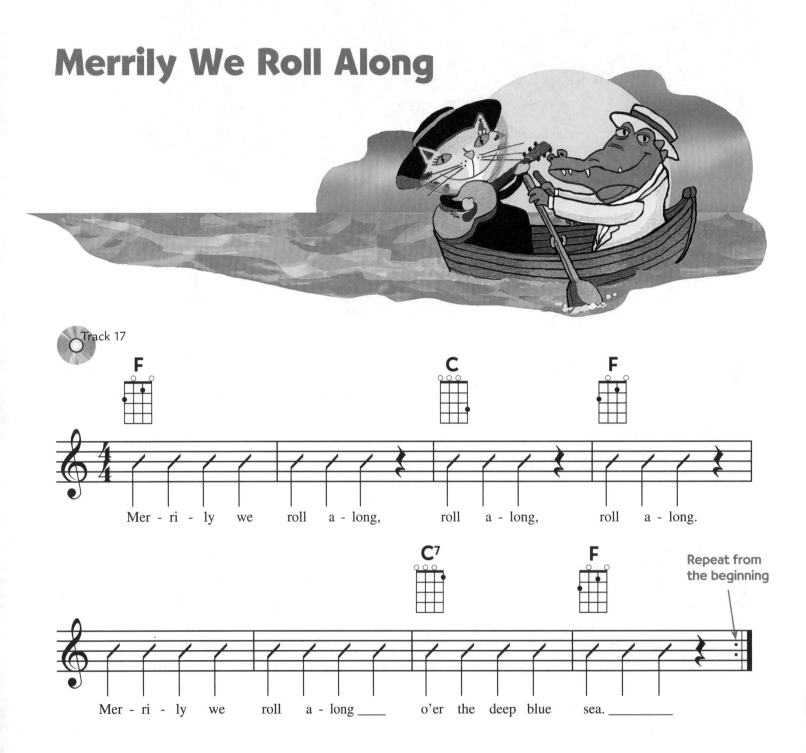

Track 17

F   C   F

Mer - ri - ly we roll a - long, roll a - long, roll a - long.

C7   F   Repeat from the beginning

Mer - ri - ly we roll a - long ____ o'er the deep blue sea. ____

18

Love Somebody

Track 18

1. Love some-bod-y, yes I do! ___ Love some-bod-y, won't say who. ___
2. Love some-bod-y, want to hear? ___ Let me whis-per in your ear. ___

Love some-bod-y, can you guess? ___ Who's the one that I love best?
Love some-bod-y, now you've guessed ___ You're the one that I love best!

19

The G⁷ Chord

Hear this chord!

Track 19

Use finger 1 to press the 2nd string at the 1st fret. Use fingers 2 and 3 to press the 3rd and 1st strings at the 2nd fret.

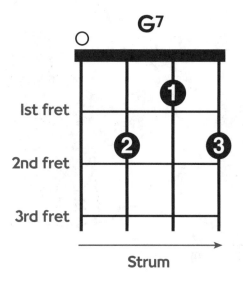

G⁷

1st fret

2nd fret

3rd fret

Strum

My Fourth Chord

Track 20

G⁷

For G sev - en, use three fing - ers.

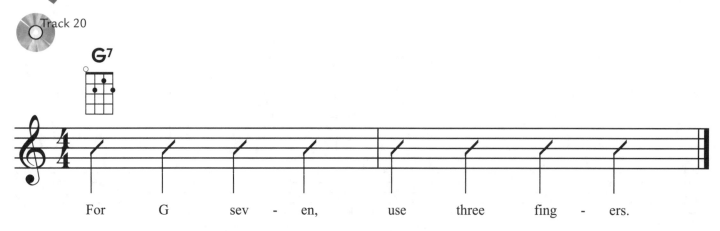

20

Using G⁷ with Other Chords

Practice Tip

Before you play "A-Tisket, A-Tasket," "Aloha 'Oe," "When the Saints Go Marching In," and "Yankee Doodle," practice the exercises on this page. They will help you to change chords easily.

Play each exercise very slowly at first, and gradually play them faster. Don't move on to play the songs until you can easily move from chord to chord without missing a beat.

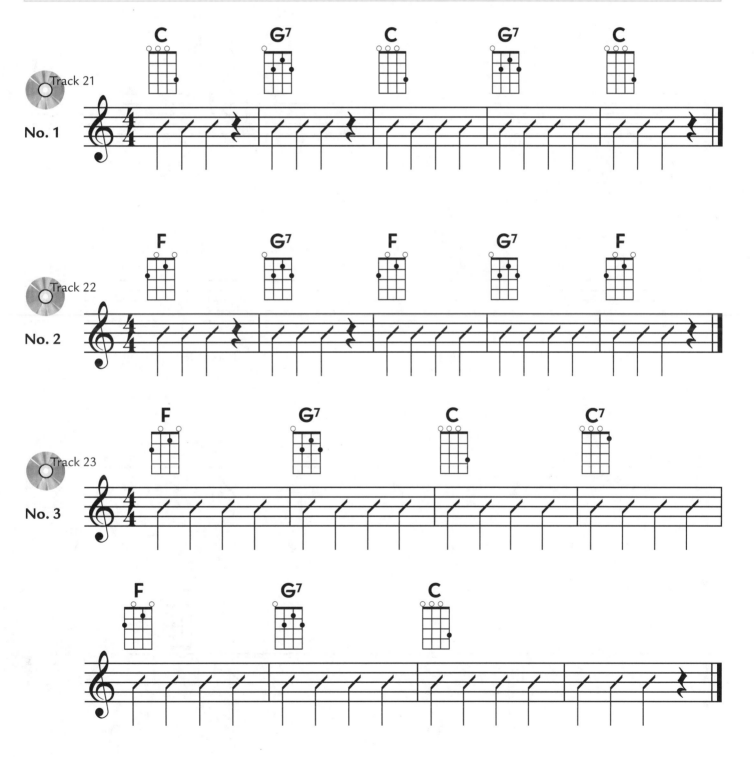

A-Tisket, A-Tasket

Track 24

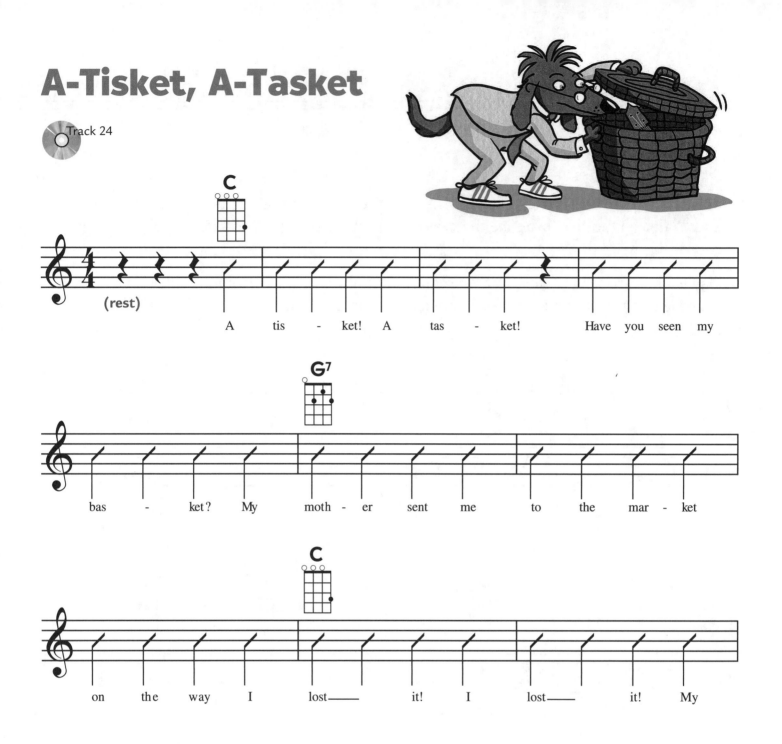

(rest)

A tis - ket! A tas - ket! Have you seen my

bas - ket? My moth - er sent me to the mar - ket

on the way I lost—— it! I lost—— it! My

bas - ket! Have you seen my bas - ket? For

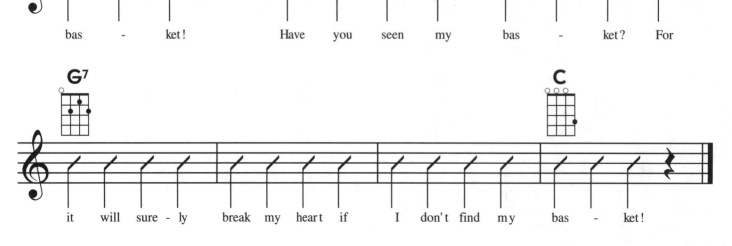

it will sure - ly break my heart if I don't find my bas - ket!

22

Aloha 'Oe
(Farewell to Thee)

Track 25

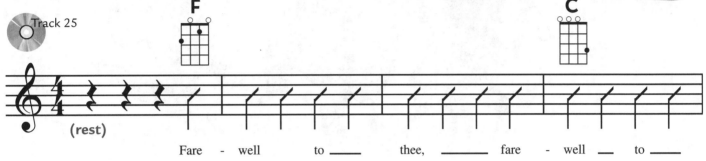

(rest)   Fare - well   to ____ thee, ____ fare - well __ to ____

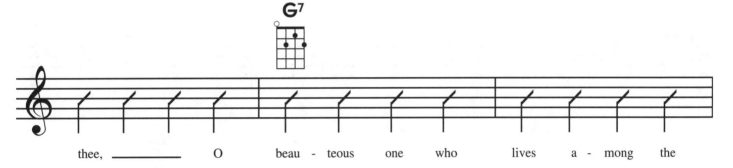

thee, _____ O   beau - teous   one   who   lives   a - mong   the

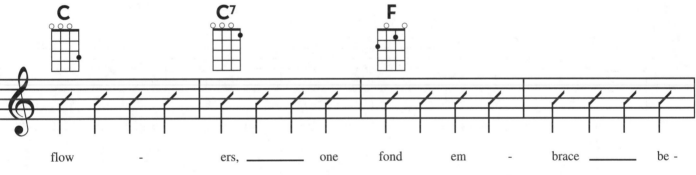

flow ____ ers, _____ one   fond   em - brace ____ be -

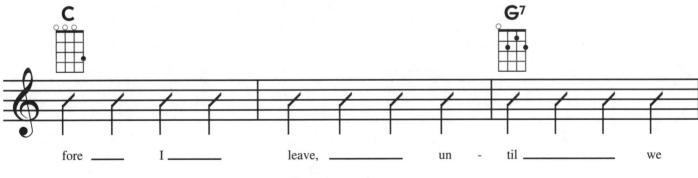

fore ____ I ____ leave, _____ un - til _____ we

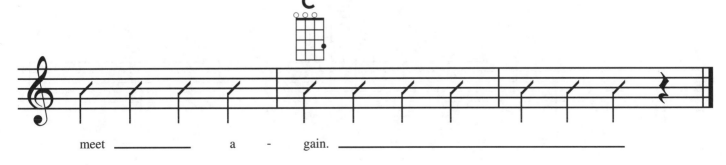

meet _____ a - gain. _____

When the Saints Go Marching In

Track 26

C

(rest) Oh when the saints go march-ing in,

G⁷

Oh when the saints go march - ing in,

C   C⁷   F

Oh how I want to be in that num - ber

C   G⁷   C

When the saints go march - ing in.

Yankee Doodle

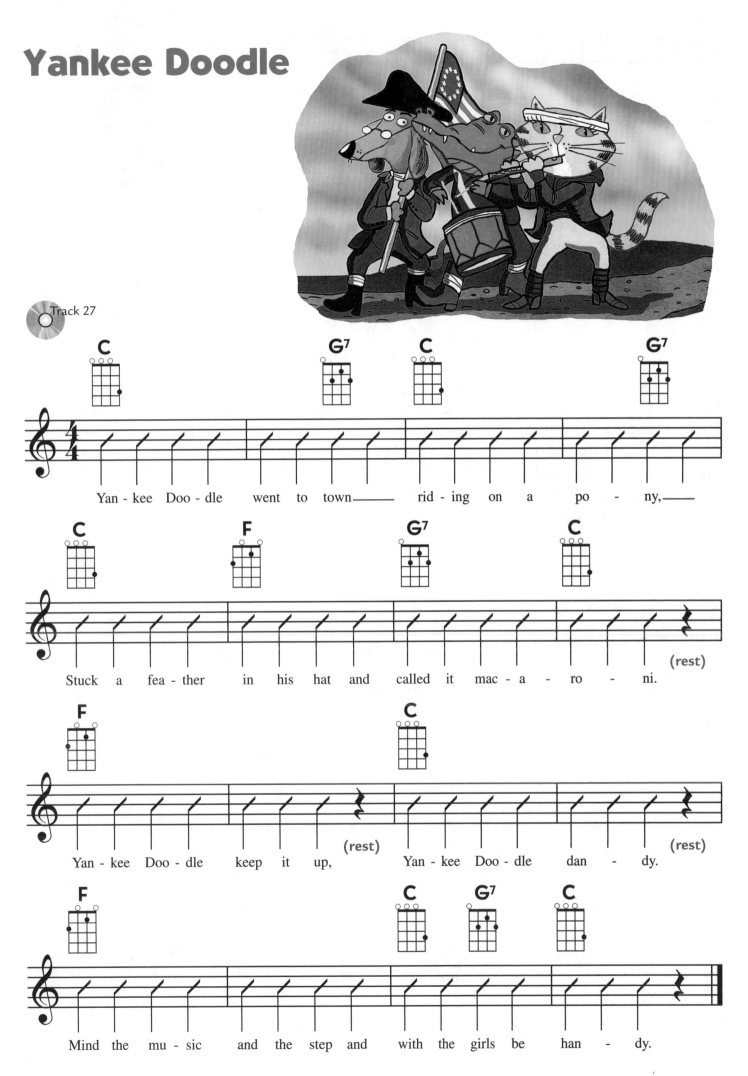

Track 27

C   **G⁷**   **C**   **G⁷**

Yan - kee Doo - dle went to town——— rid - ing on a po - ny,———

C   **F**   **G⁷**   **C**

Stuck a fea - ther in his hat and called it mac - a - ro - ni. (rest)

F   **C**

Yan - kee Doo - dle keep it up, (rest) Yan - kee Doo - dle dan - dy. (rest)

F   **C**   **G⁷**   **C**

Mind the mu - sic and the step and with the girls be han - dy.

25

Getting Acquainted with Music Notation

Notes

Musical sounds are represented by symbols called *notes*. Their time value is determined by their color (black or white), and by stems and flags attached to them.

The Staff

Each note has a name. That name depends on where the note is found on the *staff*. The staff is made up of five horizontal lines and the spaces between those lines.

5th LINE	
4th LINE	4th SPACE
3rd LINE	3rd SPACE
2nd LINE	2nd SPACE
1st LINE	1st SPACE

The Music Alphabet

The notes are named after the first seven letters of the alphabet (A–G).

A   B   C   D   E   F   G

Clefs

As music notation progressed through history, the staff had from two to twenty lines, and symbols were invented that would always give you a reference point for all the other notes. These symbols were called *clefs*.

Music for the ukulele is written in the G or *treble clef*. Originally, the Gothic letter G was used on a four-line staff to show the pitch G.

This developed into the modern clef:

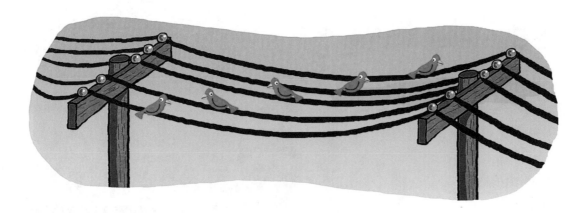

An easy way to remember the notes on the lines is using the phrase **E**very **G**ood **B**ird **D**oes **F**ly. Remembering the notes in the spaces is even easier because they spell the word **FACE**, which rhymes with "space."

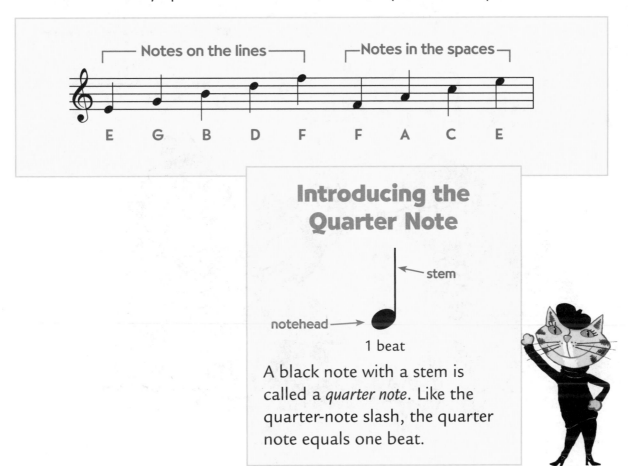

Notes on the lines

Notes in the spaces

E   G   B   D   F   F   A   C   E

Introducing the Quarter Note

stem

notehead

1 beat

A black note with a stem is called a *quarter note*. Like the quarter-note slash, the quarter note equals one beat.

Track 28

Clap and Count out Loud

$\frac{4}{4}$ ♩ ♩ ♩ ♩ | ♩ ♩ ♩ 𝄽 | ♩ ♩ ♩ 𝄽 | ♩ ♩ ♩ 𝄽 ‖

1   2   3   4   1   2   3   (4)   1   2   3   (4)   1   2   3   (4)

Notes on the First String
Introducing A

Hear this note!

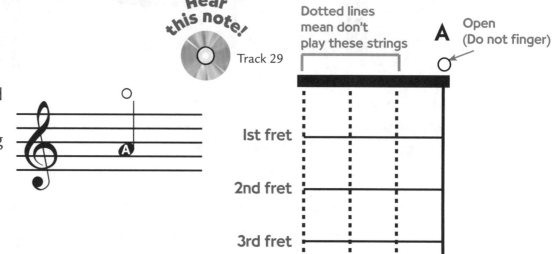

Track 29

A note sitting on the second space of the treble clef staff is called A. To play this note, pick the open 1st string (meaning without putting a left-hand finger on it).

Dotted lines mean don't play these strings

A Open (Do not finger)

1st fret
2nd fret
3rd fret

Abby, the Armadillo

Track 30

Picking

- Play each A slowly and evenly, using a *downpick* motion. We will use only downpicks for the rest of the book.

- Use only a little motion to pick each note, just like strumming.

Count:	1	2	3	4	1	2	3	4	1	2	3	4	1	2	3	4
	Al	li	ga	tor	Al	ate	ap	ples	a	round	Ab	by	Ar	ma	dil	lo.

The Note A with Chords

Practice Tip

For this tune, remember that both the F and C⁷ chords use finger 1 at the 1st fret.

F Chord

C⁷ Chord

It's easy to move your finger over one string to change chords, but don't forget your 2nd finger on the 4th string.

Track 31

Note and Strum Warm-up

Before playing "Note and Strum" practice this exercise slowly until you are comfortable playing a note followed by a strum.

Note and Strum

Track 32

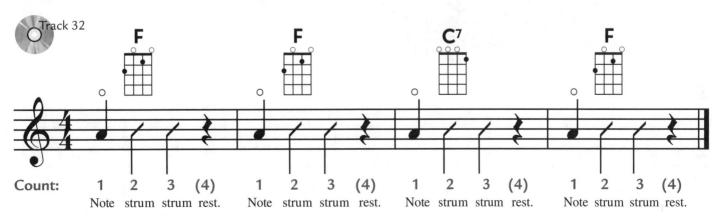

Notes on the First String
Introducing B

Hear this note! Track 33

A note on the middle line of the staff is called B. To play this note, use finger 2 to press the 1st string at the 2nd fret. Use a downpick motion to play only the 1st string.

B

1st fret

2nd fret — Second finger — ②

3rd fret

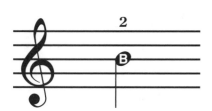

Up-Down-Up

Track 34

Up-Down-Up Warm-up

Before playing "Up-Down-Up," practice this exercise until you are comfortable playing the note B.

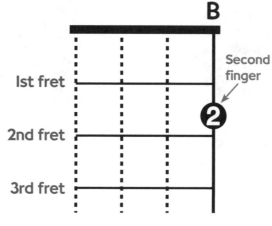

Track 35

Start on A then se - cond fin - ger. Down to A then up to the B.

The Notes A and B with Chords

Practice Tip

For this tune, notice that the note B and the C chord are one finger apart. Finger the B with the 2nd finger on the 2nd fret of the 1st string, and then use the 3rd finger on the 3rd fret of the 1st string to play the C chord. First, just practice switching those fingers and then play the music below.

Note B

C Chord

Track 36

A strum strum rest. B strum strum rest. One more time rest, then you can rest.

31

Notes on the First String
Introducing C

Hear this note!

Track 37

A note sitting on the third space of the treble clef staff is called C. Use finger 3 to press the 1st string at the 3rd fret. Use a downpick motion to play only the 1st string.

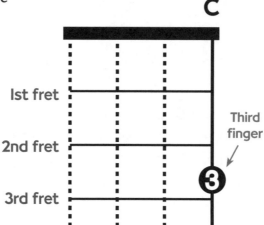

C

1st fret

2nd fret

3rd fret

Third finger

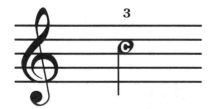

Track 38

C Warm-up

The Mountain Climber

Track 39

From the bot - tom to the top, the fear - less climb - er does not stop.

With his fav - 'rite uke he seeks to yo - del from the moun - tain peaks.

The Notes A, B, and C with Chords

Practice Tip

Notice that the note C and the C chord are both fingered with finger 3 at the 3rd fret on the 1st string.

Note C

C Chord

Hold down the 3rd finger between the note C and the C chord.

Brave in the Cave

Track 40

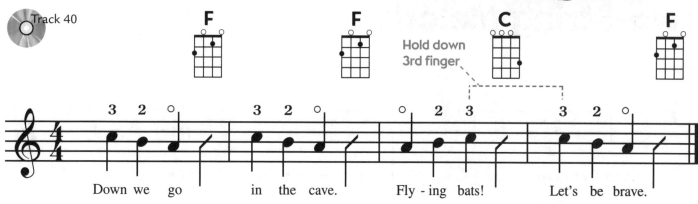

Down we go in the cave. Fly - ing bats! Let's be brave.

33

Notes on the Second String
Introducing E

Hear this note! Track 41

A note on the lowest line of the staff is called E. Play the 2nd string open.

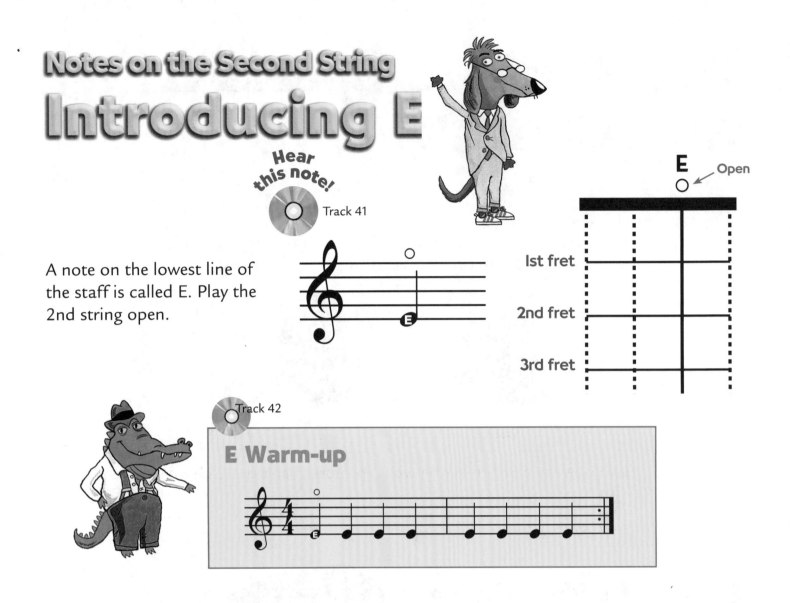

Track 42

E Warm-up

Two Open Strings

Track 43

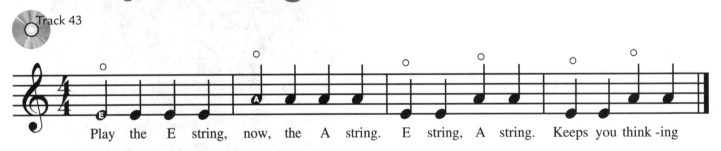

Play the E string, now, the A string. E string, A string. Keeps you think -ing

Two-String Melody

Track 44

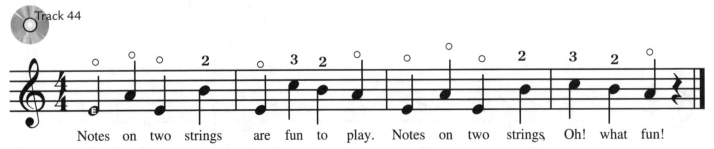

Notes on two strings are fun to play. Notes on two strings, Oh! what fun!

Jumping Around

Track 45

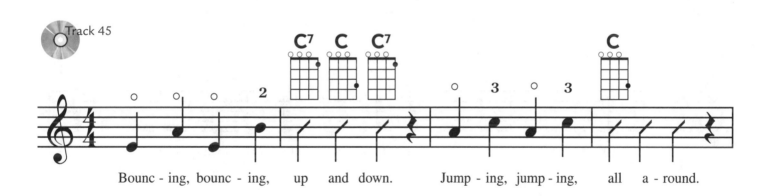

Bounc - ing, bounc - ing, up and down. Jump - ing, jump - ing, all a - round.

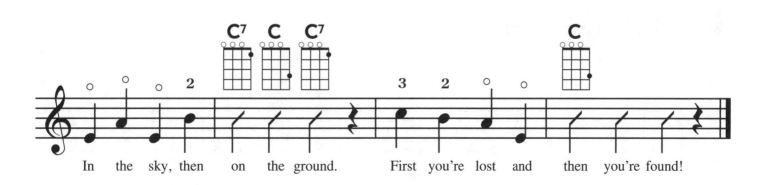

In the sky, then on the ground. First you're lost and then you're found!

Notes on the Second String
Introducing F

Hear this note! Track 46

A note on the 1st space of the staff is called F. Use finger 1 to press the 2nd string at the 1st fret. Pick only the 2nd string.

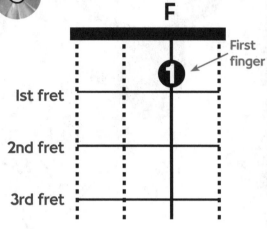

F

1st fret

2nd fret

3rd fret

First finger

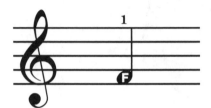

Track 47

F Warm-up

Ping Pong Song

Track 48

O - pen E string, first fin - ger F, down to E then up to F.

Soccer Game

Track 49

Hold

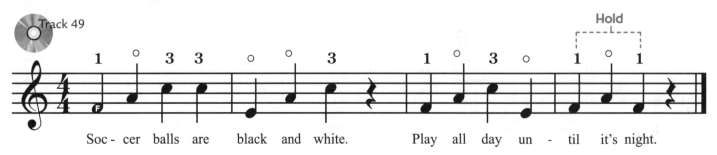

Soc - cer balls are black and white. Play all day un - til it's night.

The Half Rest

Introducing the Half Rest

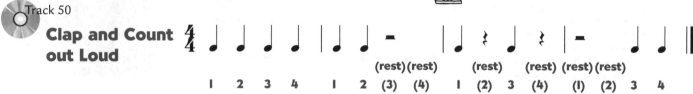

This rest means do not play for two beats, which is the same as 𝄽 𝄽 .

Track 50

Clap and Count out Loud

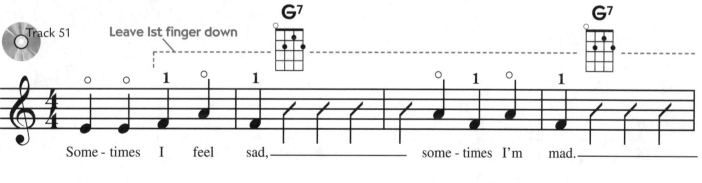

1 2 3 4   1 2 (3) (4)   1 (2) 3 (4)   (1) (2) 3 4
                 (rest)(rest)   (rest) (rest)   (rest)(rest)

Practice Tip

Notice that the note F and the G⁷ chord are both fingered with finger 1 at the 1st fret on the 2nd string.

In "When I Feel Best," hold the 1st finger down from the third beat of the 1st measure until the last beat of the 5th measure.

Note F

G⁷ Chord

When I Feel Best

Track 51

Some - times I feel sad,———— some - times I'm mad.

—— But I feel best at all the times that I feel glad.——

37

Notes on the Second String
Introducing G

Hear this note! Track 52

A note on the 2nd line of the staff is called G. Use finger 3 to press the 2nd string at the 3rd fret. Pick only the 2nd string.

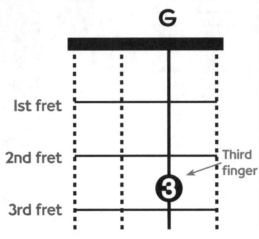

G

1st fret

2nd fret — Third finger

3rd fret

Track 53

G Warm-up

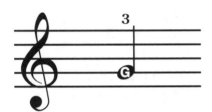

A-Choo!

Track 54

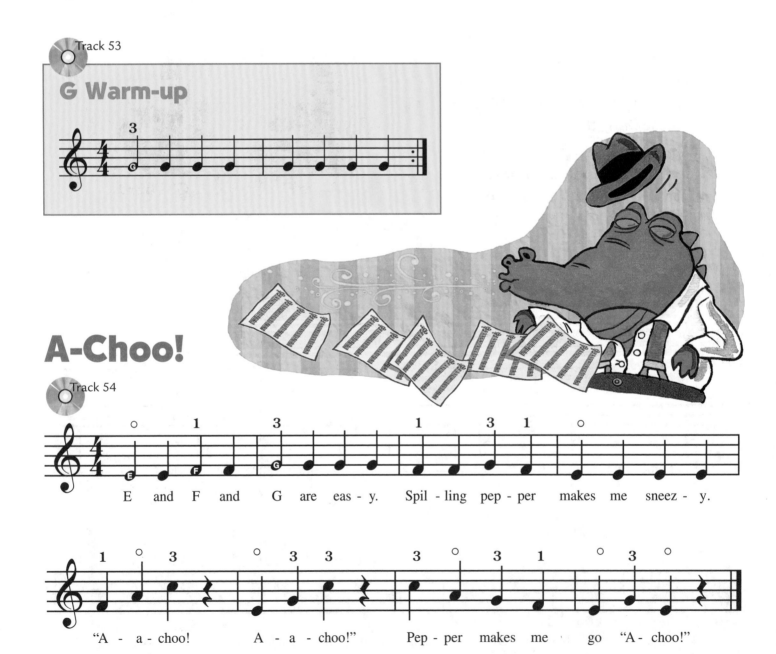

E and F and G are eas-y. Spil-ling pep-per makes me sneez-y.

"A - a - choo! A - a - choo!" Pep-per makes me go "A-choo!"

The Half Note

Introducing the Half Note

2 beats

This note lasts two beats.
It is twice as long as a quarter note.

Track 55

Clap and Count out Loud

1 2 3 4   1 2 3 4   1 2 3 4   1 2 3 4

Hot Cross Buns

Track 56

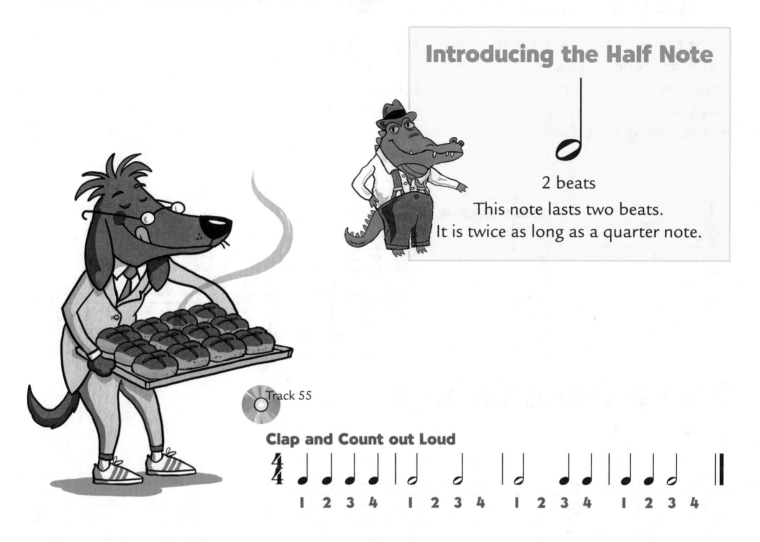

Count: 1   2   3   4   1   2   (3) (4)   1   2   3   4   1   2   (3) (4)
Hot   cross   buns,   hot   cross   buns,

Keep Counting!   One a pen - ny,   two a pen - ny,   hot cross buns.

39

Notes on the Third String
Introducing C

A line that extends the staff either up or down is called a *ledger line*. A note one ledger line below the staff is called C. You already know C on the 1st string. This C is the open 3rd string and sounds lower than C on the 1st string. To play this note, pick the open 3rd string.

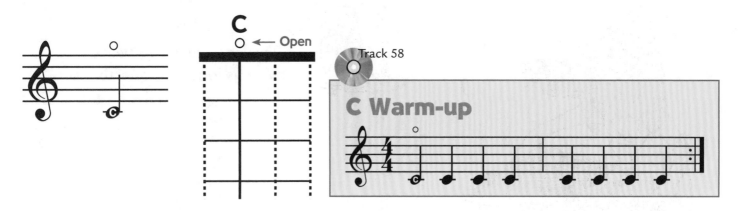

C
← Open

Track 58

C Warm-up

Three Open Strings

Track 59

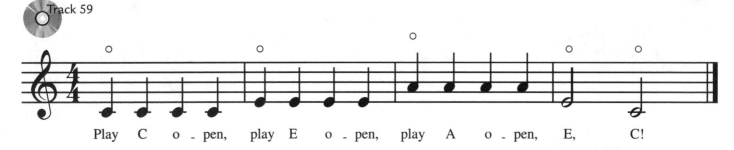

Play C o - pen, play E o - pen, play A o - pen, E, C!

Little Steps and Big Leaps

Track 60

Play - ing on three strings lets me play notes far a - part.

Lit - tle steps and big leaps make my play - ing like fine art.

40

The Old Grey Mare

Track 61

(rest) The old grey mare she ain't what she

used to be, ain't what she used to be, ain't what she

used to be, The old grey mare she ain't what she

used to be, man - y long years a - go. _____

F

Notes on the Third String
Introducing D

Hear this note!  Track 62

A note on the space below the staff is called D. Use finger 2 to press the 3rd string at the 2nd fret. Pick only the 3rd string.

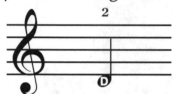

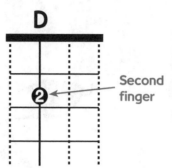

D — Second finger

Introducing the Whole Note

This note lasts four beats. It is as long as two half notes, or four quarter notes.

o 4 beats

Track 63

D Warm-up

Clap and Count out Loud

Track 64

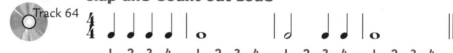

1 2 3 4   1 2 3 4   1 2 3 4   1 2 3 4

D Is Easy! Track 65

D is eas - y   if   you   place   your   sec - ond   fin - ger   on   the   C   string.

Taking a Walk   Track 66

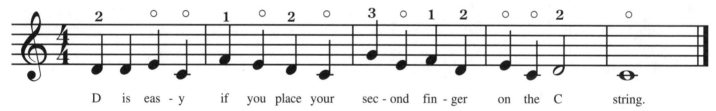

Walk - ing   up   to   G,   then   walk   down   to   C.

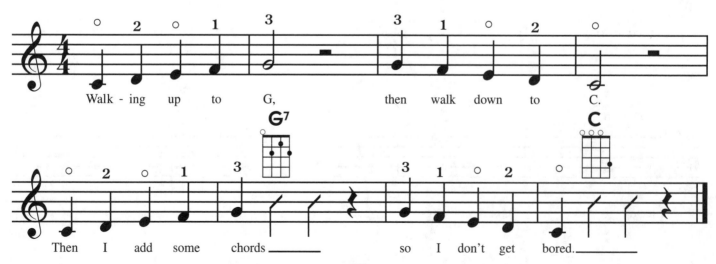

G⁷   **C**

Then   I   add   some   chords ____   so   I   don't   get   bored. ____

Ode to Joy
from Beethoven's 9th Symphony

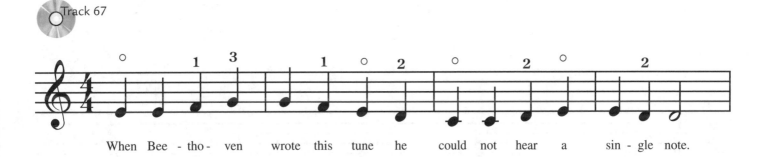

Track 67

When Bee - tho - ven wrote this tune he could not hear a sin - gle note.

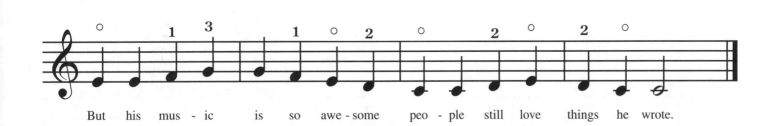

But his mus - ic is so awe - some peo - ple still love things he wrote.

Jingle Bells

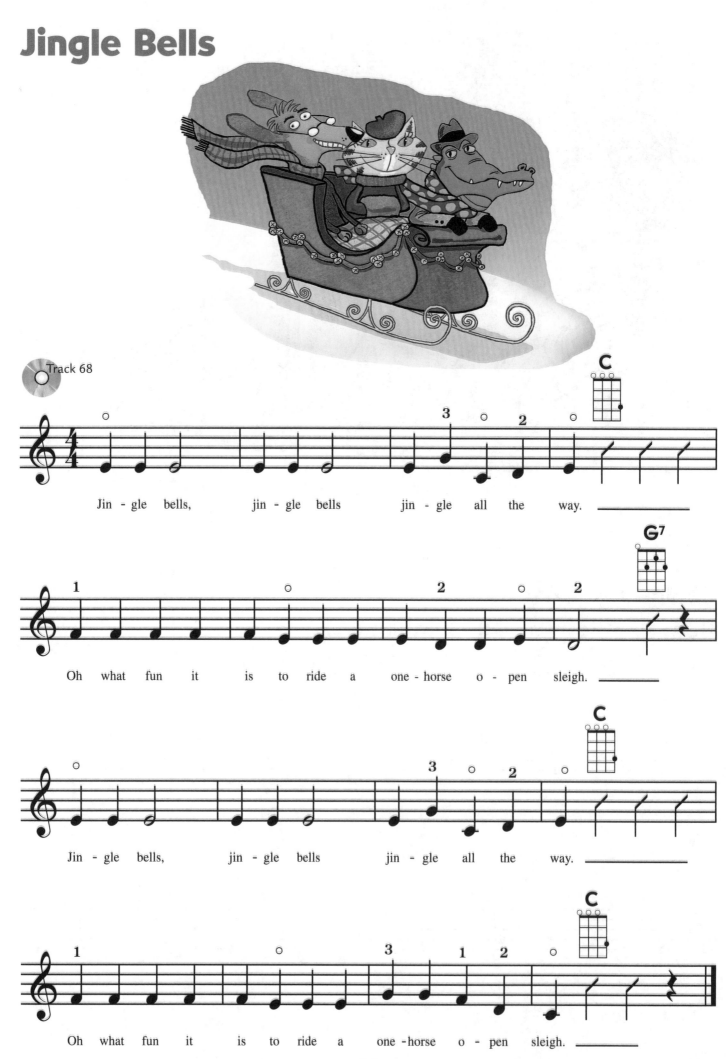

Track 68

C

Jin - gle bells,   jin - gle bells   jin - gle all   the   way. _____

G⁷

Oh what fun   it   is   to   ride   a   one - horse o - pen sleigh. _____

C

Jin - gle bells,   jin - gle bells   jin - gle all   the   way. _____

C

Oh what fun   it   is   to   ride   a   one - horse o - pen sleigh. _____

Mary Had a Little Lamb

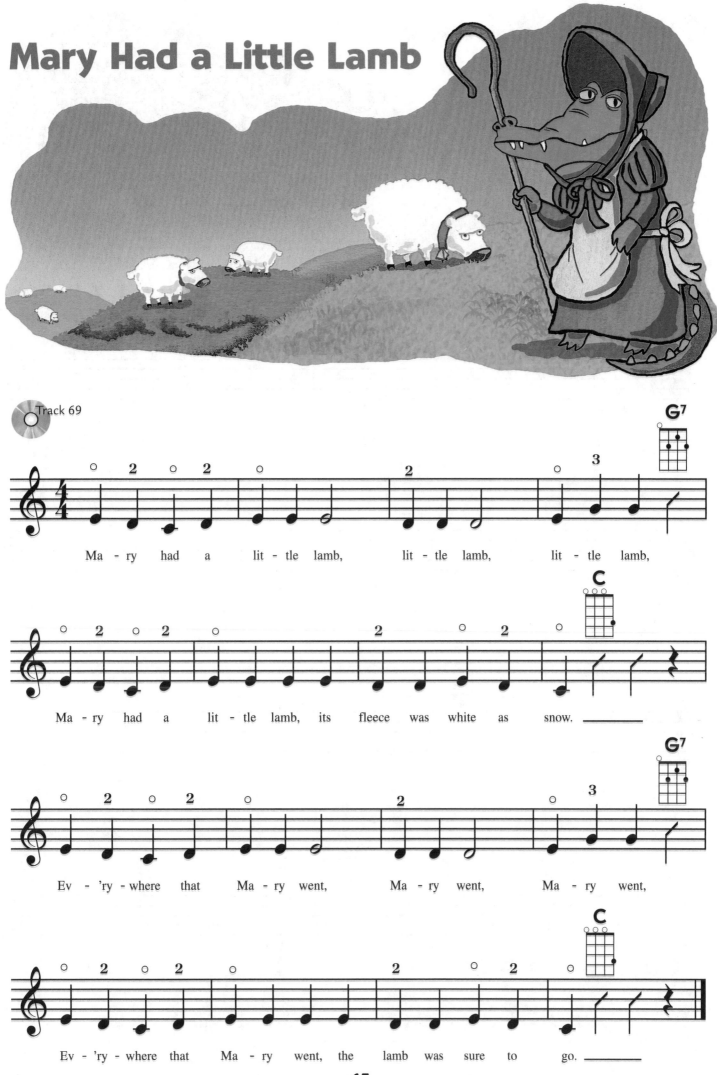

Track 69

Ma - ry had a lit - tle lamb, lit - tle lamb, lit - tle lamb,

Ma - ry had a lit - tle lamb, its fleece was white as snow. ____

Ev - 'ry - where that Ma - ry went, Ma - ry went, Ma - ry went,

Ev - 'ry - where that Ma - ry went, the lamb was sure to go. ____

Over the Rainbow

Track 70

Words by E. Y. Harburg
Music by Harold Arlen

Some - where _____ o - ver the rain - bow

way _____ up _____ high, _____

there's _____ a _____ land that I heard of once in a

lul - la - by. _____

Music Matching Games

Chords

Draw a line to match each chord frame on the left to the correct photo on the right.

1.

2.

3.

4.

Symbols

Draw a line to match each symbol on the left to its name on the right.

1. o   Treble clef

2.   Quarter note

3.   Whole note

4.   Quarter slash

5.   Half note

6.   Double bar line

7.   Half rest

8.   Repeat sign

9.   Quarter rest

Notes

Draw a line to match each note on the left to its correct music notation on the right.

1.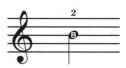

2.

3.

4.

5.

6.

7.

8.

Answer Key

Chords
1: page 14; 2: page 12; 3: page 10; 4: page 20

Symbols
1: page 42; 2: page 39; 3: page 27; 4: page 8;
5: page 26; 6: page 18; 7: page 37; 8: page 11;
9: page 8

Notes
1: page 28; 2: page 30; 3: page 32; 4: page 34;
5: page 36; 6: page 38; 7: page 40; 8: page 42

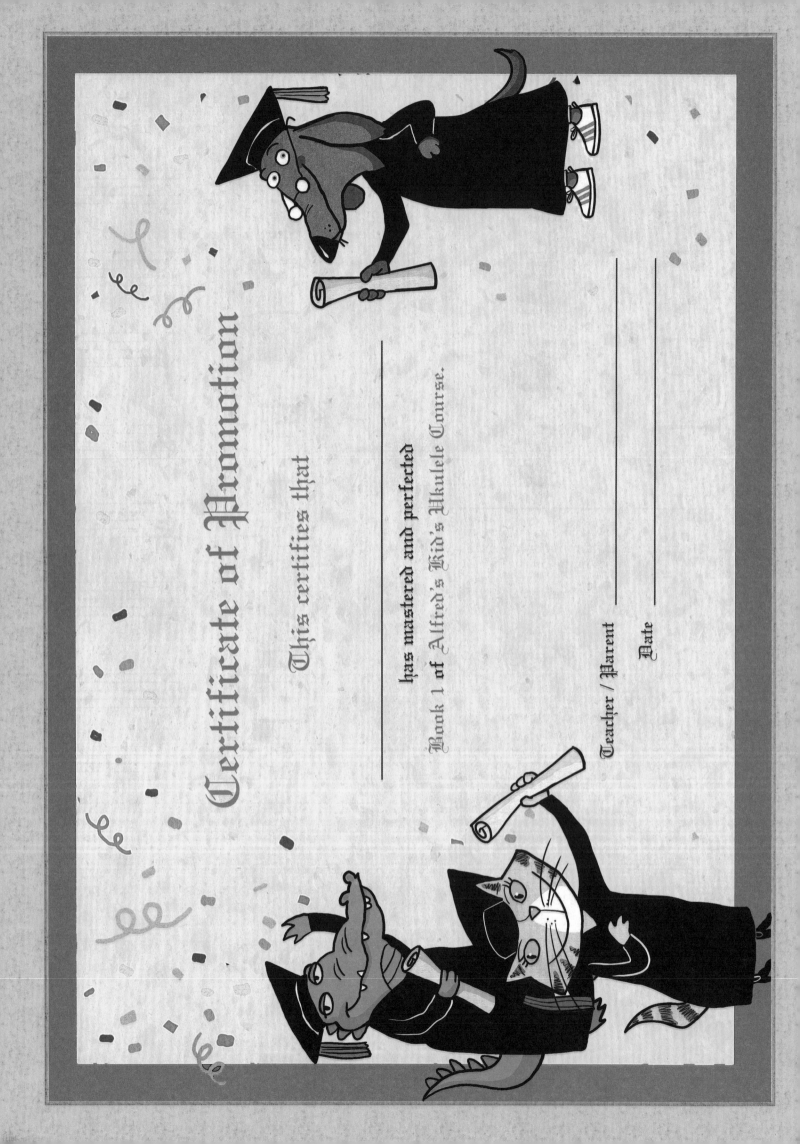

Certificate of Promotion

This certifies that

_____

has mastered and perfected

_____

Book 1 of Alfred's Kid's Ukulele Course.

_____
Teacher / Parent

_____
Date